The Gift of Christmas Present

Advent Devotions for Regaining Hope, Peace, Love and Joy

By Keri Wyatt Kent

The Gift Of Christmas Present

Copyright 2022 Keri Wyatt Kent
Published by A Powerful Story
Hoffman Estates, IL

Revised for 2022
www.APowerfulStory.com

Cover design by Tommy Owen
Interior design by Carol Davis

Printed in the United States of America

All rights reserved. No part of this publication may be reproduced, stored in a retrieval system, or transmitted in any form or by any means—for example, electronic, photocopy, recording—without the prior written permission of the publisher.

The only exception is brief quotations in printed reviews.

Scripture marked MSG is taken from The Message by Eugene H. Peterson, copyright © 1993, 1994, 1995, 2000, 2001, 2002. Used by permission of NavPress Publishing Group. All rights reserved.

Scripture marked NIV is taken from the THE HOLY BIBLE, NEW INTERNATIONAL VERSION®, NIV® Copyright © 1973, 1978, 1984, 2011 by Biblica, Inc.® Used by permission. All rights reserved worldwide.

Scripture marked NLT is taken from the Holy Bible, New Living Translation, copyright © 1996. Used by permission of Tyndale House Publishers, Inc., Wheaton, Illinois 60189. All rights reserved.

ISBN 979-8-9853052-0-3

Introduction

There is a deep longing in our hearts, which the season of Advent intensifies. The longing is for presence, for meaning, for connection. With God, with others, with our own inner self.

The words of the prophet Isaiah resonate: the people walking in darkness have seen a great light. We are hoping to God it's true, that the darkness is giving way, that the light of hope really is on the horizon.

If you are reading this, you are a survivor. You've survived a pandemic, not to mention chaos, vitriol and other traumas. In this post-traumatic state, restoration comes from acknowledging the struggles and stresses, then leaning into the source of healing: the Christmas child.

This time of year, in our culture, can be stressful. The thing is, right now, we don't need more stress. In fact, just preparing for the holidays may feel triggering. Our souls are hungry for hope. We crave peace. We want to give and receive love, more than any material thing. We're longing for joy. These four—hope, peace, love, and joy—are traditional themes of Advent, the season just before Christmas.

When Jo Robinson and Jean Saeheli, authors of *Unplug The Christmas Machine,* asked women to describe the Christmas season in three words, the responses they received were telling. Off the top of their heads, women came up with combinations like:

- rushed, overwhelmed, joy
- gifts, tree, stressful
- travel, excited, worried

We're obviously a little conflicted. Throw in the pressures of a world completely upended by a pandemic, and we may find ourselves with more stress and less joy. And yet, we long for a meaningful Advent season.

Insanity begins to happen when the gap between your expectations and your reality gets too wide. This month, that gap expands—especially for women, who despite the progress we've made culturally, still often consider Christmas our personal responsibility. Unless, that is, we decide to choose a different path. To live intentionally. To be fully present.

Over the next four weeks, you're invited to reflect on the coming of Jesus, who brought these gifts and more into our weary world. To let go of expectations and trying to do too much, so that you can open your hands to the gift of Christmas present.

Psychologists tell us that "stress contagion" happens when one person's tension spreads to the people around them. We see this happen at work, in families, even with strangers. Kids not only catch our stress, they add to it. Advertising brainwashes them into tiny dictator consumers.

We may think we're hiding our struggles. (I'm fine, really. This twitch? It will go away in January.) But we are not fooling anyone. Our body language, voices and faces show the stress, reveal the fact that the gap between our reality and our ideals gets very wide in December.

We say we want to be compassionate, but we get competitive. We say we want to focus on our priorities, but instead we become perfectionists. We say we want to look for true meaning, but we get up at 4 a.m. to get in line to drop $120 on whatever toy or gadget the advertising industry has convinced us, or the aforementioned tiny dictators, is indispensable and must be obtained and placed under our Christmas tree.

More than any time of year, the holidays are a time when focusing on the moment feels impossible. We've got Pinterest pins and voice memos and hastily jotted notes on the margin of the Wal-Mart Christmas flyer, reminding us of all the things we have to do and buy and *curate* in the next four weeks. We're shopping, wrapping, planning, decorating. While trying to keep up with work or our families and the normal juggling we do 365 days a year.

Yet no matter how much we do or buy or plan, we wrestle with some guilt, because we think we're supposed to focus the spiritual meaning of a religious holiday. The layered obligations and conflicting goals add up to stress, and even burnout.

The obvious question about the holiday season, the season of Advent, is why? Why, when we want to focus on deeper things, do we get distracted by the superficial?

During this special time of year, fueled by too many hours of Pinterest and HGTV, we get obsessed with decorating and crafts and cooking—even if we normally don't really enjoy those activities. We want to bake perfect cookies, set a perfect table, find the perfect gift, drop the perfect hint for the gift we hope to get…

Why does Christmas become a competition? What is it that we are trying to "win"? What is it that we are really seeking? Maybe: significance.

Which is not a bad thing to want. You were created for significance—in fact, you're deeply loved and you already have significance. How much time do you spend seeking what you already have? You already have it—even if you don't feel or recognize it yet. You don't need to seek significance in things that cannot actually give it: accomplishments, busyness, stuff.

Our desire for significance might be fueling our crazy plans for cookies, decorating, gifts, parties. We want that cozy holiday feeling, we want to know that we created that wonderful moment, that amazing memory, that magical Christmas morning--and we make ourselves and everyone around us crazy trying to achieve it. But, instead of cozy, we feel pressure. Instead of joy, we feel stress. We're overwhelmed.

A lot of this is about our need to be okay, or even, amazing. The truth is, we want to win. We want to win Christmas. After last year, when many of us had to forgo gathering, there's a pressure to make this year better than ever.

How can we regain our sanity? Well, I can't promise you complete calm during the holiday season, but I do want to give you a gift: the gift of Christmas present. It's actually a gift I want to guide you toward giving to yourself.

This devotional can help you to pause, for just five minutes a day, to slow down, to dial in to what you most want: a meaningful Christmas season. And that five minutes can help recalibrate and reconnect you to the four themes of Advent: hope, peace, love, and joy. It will give you some quiet thoughts to hang on to during your day, to help you to slow down and be fully present.

Our stressful state comes directly from our hurried lives. We're hurried, busy, overwhelmed. This amps up during the holidays. But our stress is less about our circumstances, and more about how we *think about* our circumstances.

Unfortunately, we don't interpret accurately when we're hurried. And we're hurried when we are thinking about the past or the future, instead of the present moment. One way to reduce your stress is to simply notice, what am I thinking about? Am I thinking about the past, even ten minutes ago, or the future, what's going to happen, what you have to do? Or am I fully present right now, paying attention to myself and to others? Am I distracted or attentive?

Haunted by Past and Future

When we are haunted by Christmas Past, or Christmas Future, we cannot receive Christmas Present.

Some of us are stuck in Christmas past. We re-live past burned turkeys or gift flops, and worry we won't get it right. Or we remember past disappointments or criticisms. Our holiday memories are painful, but we can't let go of them. Our fragile heart says, "I remember this season. It's the one where I always get hurt, where I have felt deeply disappointed."

We focus on the past and try to revise it—which is impossible. We vow that this year will be different. We're trying so hard and yet it never seems to be enough.

Maybe you're just trying to survive a time that seems to simply highlight your loneliness. Maybe this is your first Christmas without a certain person, or yet another Christmas where you are again aware of feeling lonely or left out. You're aware of what you once had, but don't any longer: a parent, a spouse, a houseful of children.

The prevailing emotion of those living in Christmas past is regret. Regret is the fear that we have messed up. Regret keeps us from experiencing the joy and peace of Christmas present.

Others of us are living in Christmas future, ruled by our to-do lists. Our primary emotion is worry. Will we get it all done? Will everyone be impressed? We are shopping, wrapping, baking, decorating. We could try to enjoy those things, but instead, we endure them, because they're a means to an end, a way to have something we believe is in our immediate future: the approval and admiration of other people, whether it's for gifts, the perfect meal, our kids being happy on Christmas morning.

Christmas feels like a race, and if we stop running, it won't happen. I remember one year, after a particularly stressful day of baking, shopping, wrapping, and planning, I told my husband, "I am making Christmas happen!"

Living in Christmas future creates a huge burden, made heavier by our resentment. We focus on tasks rather than people, but get mad when people don't appreciate our efforts. We set ourselves up for failure, exhaustion, or both. We can't enjoy the present moment because we have too much to do and no one to help us. Why isn't anyone helping us? Maybe it's because we've made it clear that they can't do it right so they might as well not try. Or maybe, we simply haven't asked for help, and other people assume we're having fun doing everything.

It is hard, all year long, to be present. That is, to focus on the moment you are in right now, instead of regretting about the past: mistakes you've made, things that didn't get done; or worrying about the future: things that you have to do, upcoming tasks or gatherings.

Focusing on the future or the past will make you feel hurried. Focusing on the present will help you to slow down, calm down, feel more content. Have you ever had a conversation with someone who was obviously thinking about something else? That something else is often the past, or the future. That keeps them from being fully present with you. Maybe you've been that person, who is not fully present.

Contrast that with someone who is fully present, totally attentive, actually listening.

This time of year, it's hard to be present. Which is ironic, because it's a time we talk about presents a lot. But the one thing we forget to give ourselves, and the people around us, is the gift of being present, of being mindful, paying attention, being in the moment.

If the past few years has taught us anything, it's this: you can make all kinds of plans, but really, very little is within our control. Or as the Bible says, We can make our plans, but the LORD determines our steps. (See Proverbs 16:9)

So as we look forward to the holidays, we may do so with some trepidation. Will we be able to gather with family? Can we invite the neighbors in for a cup of tea and some Christmas cookies? Do we have to bake those cookies?

How to use this book

This devotional will keep you centered during this busy time of year. This year, we need that centering more than ever. We need the gift of Christmas present. This book is an invitation to savor the season—without feeling like it's another thing on your to-do list. What if you gave yourself just five minutes a day to slow down, reflect and pray?

This year, let's walk together through the Advent season. Advent means coming—we're anticipating the coming of Jesus, the birth of the Messiah, and also, his future return. If it's helpful, you can light the candles in an Advent wreath, but don't feel you have to. Traditionally, the four weeks of Advent focus on four themes: hope, peace, love and joy. These will provide a framework for our journey together.

Each day, you'll read a verse. Don't skip the Scripture (you know we all do it)! Stop, read slow, reflect. Be fully present, listening to God speak through the words on the page. If that's all you have time for, that's enough. But if you want to give yourself a gift, keep going.

Read the short reflection that follows each Scripture. Each day also offers a journaling question, and a prayer. These are tools, use them or don't, but take some time each day to pray and reflect. That simple practice: read, reflect, journal, pray, can slow you down a little. And slowing down helps us to be present, to live in the moment instead of the future or the past.

What would happen if you were to slow down enough to be present during the next four weeks? Being present is a gift you can give to yourself, and to others. Our tendency to cling to the regrets of the past, or worry about the future, is driven by fear. Too often, we listen the voice of fear, and it drowns out the voice of love that would keep us in the present. When we live in Christmas present, we let go of regret about the past, and worry about the future, and we experience peace.

Is the emotion underlying your holiday stress actually fear? We think we just need to power up, to be brave, courageous. But the Bible says the opposite of fear is love. Love helps us be brave. Slowing down helps us to breathe and live courageously. And this resource can help you listen to the voice of love, for just a few minutes each day.

Week One

Traditionally, the first week of Advent focuses on the theme of Hope. The Bible says, "Now faith is confidence in what we hope for and assurance about what we do not see" (Hebrews 1:11). Hope might seem to be in short supply this year. What are you hoping for? How can we keep hope alive?

November 27

Give thanks for everything to God the Father in the name of our Lord Jesus Christ. (Ephesians 5:20, NIV)

A few days ago, we celebrated Thanksgiving. What did you give thanks for?

When we stop and take stock of things, breathe for a moment and remember that all is gift, doesn't it ignite just a little bit of hope in our hearts?

Maybe just the fact that you're able to gather with a few friends or family is enough—we remember the recent past, when many of us gathered only over Zoom.

Thanksgiving is one of my favorite holidays, because I love to gather friends and family and feed them. Hospitality is my jam. A day focused on gratitude, good food and people around my table? What's not to love? I feel grateful when I gather people and feed them.

How does gratitude intersect with hope? Gratitude is the path to hope, and faith. We can't just force faith, muster up hope. But we can choose gratitude. If we make gratitude our daily practice, we will find our outlook on life to be more hopeful. We will notice more specifically what God has done, what blessings flow in our lives.

Journal: Stop, breathe, and take stock. What are you thankful for?

Pray: God you are good. In spite of the hard things in my life, I am grateful for your presence in my life. Give me strength for the challenges, and open my eyes to the blessings.

November 28

So, my very dear friends, don't get thrown off course. Every desirable and beneficial gift comes out of heaven. The gifts are rivers of light cascading down from the Father of Light. (James 1:16-17, MSG)

This week, you'll be assaulted, confronted, or at least cajoled. Materialism, disguised as a way to show love, will be in your face. Our culture declares this week to be not the beginning of Advent, but the launch of Holiday Shopping Season.

Friends, don't let your desire to focus on the true meaning of the season get thrown off course. Don't get distracted and think the stuff, the décor, the "just right thing" are what matters. Because it's not about stuff.

In the hit musical *Hamilton,* there's line, repeated in several of the songs: "Look around, look around, at how lucky we are to be alive right now."

In different scenes, the line takes on different meanings. Sometimes, it's pure gratitude and excitement to be living in such a time in history. Other times, it's more to express relief for survival.

Hope grows when we look around. Put down the phone or the sleek holiday magazine and instead, breathe. Pay attention, and notice how lucky you are to be alive right now. Every day, you get to choose gratitude.

Gratitude needs an object—someone we are grateful to, or grateful for. In this season, our gratitude is directed toward God, the giver of all good things.

Journal: What is throwing you off course today? What beneficial gifts are coming your way? Where will you focus?

Pray: Fill me with your rivers of light, God. Help me to resist the pull of materialism during this holiday season, and instead to focus on the good gifts that come from you.

November 29

Give your entire attention to what God is doing right now, and don't get worked up about what may or may not happen tomorrow. God will help you deal with whatever hard things come up when the time comes.
(Matthew 6:34, MSG)

As the days get shorter and darker, life can begin to feel darker as well. We feel pressured, overwhelmed.

Over the last few years, we've all lost something: maybe a job, maybe a loved one, certainly our "normal life" to one degree or another. In the face of this, gratitude doesn't flow naturally. It must be chosen, practiced. But when we choose it, hope blossoms.

How? Take a moment to reflect and consider—how am I blessed? There is good today, which gives us reason to believe, or hope, there will be good tomorrow.

We sometimes live waiting for the other shoe to drop, worrying about what might happen? Things might go downhill. The truth is—they might. Our circumstances can change—think about how things have changed in the past year or two.

But when we focus on the present moment, and decide to practice gratitude for it, we realize that we can't control what happened yesterday or what tomorrow will bring.

It's somewhat ironic, but our hope for the future grows when we stop trying to control the future. When we accept the things we cannot change, even as we have the courage to change the things we can.

Journal: What hard things are you facing today? What worries weigh you down? Write them down, and imagine Jesus sitting before you. Hand him the piece of paper. Remember through your day that Jesus is holding these worries, so you don't need to.

Pray: God grant me the serenity to accept the things I cannot change; the courage to change the things I can; and the wisdom to know the difference.

November 30

> *And Isaiah's word:*
> *There's the root of our ancestor Jesse,*
> *breaking through the earth and growing tree tall,*
> *Tall enough for everyone everywhere to see and take hope!*
> *Oh! May the God of green hope fill you up with joy, fill you up with peace, so that your believing lives, filled with the life-giving energy of the Holy Spirit, will brim over with hope! (Romans 15:12-13, MSG)*

Each year, we remember the birth of Jesus. In these darkening days of winter, we are hungry for the green of rebirth, of new life. We remember the hope, the promise, the longing of God's people, in the generations that waited for Messiah. It reminds us of our own longing for redemption, for that same Messiah's return.

Imagine trying to fill a cup of juice for a squirmy child. They hold it up but keep moving it, jostling it, walking away when distracted. Filling it feels impossible and potentially quite messy.

We are that impatient child: demanding to be filled but never holding our cup still for just a moment, long enough to receive what God wants to pour into our lives.

How do we access a life brimming over with hope? We cannot muster it up on our own, but we can draw near to God to be filled. The times I feel the divine presence most acutely are those when I am not worrying about the future or obsessing about past mistakes, but instead, am simply present, and still. Attending to what is right in front of me, I become aware: God is pouring out hope that fills us with peace, with joy.

Journal: What barriers get in the way of simply being still? What happens when you sit, breathe, get quiet and just listen? Try it.

Pray: God help me to be still, allowing you to fill me to overflowing with hope. Holy Spirit, pour into me your life-giving energy. Today I receive the evergreen hope of your love.

December 1

We wait in hope for the Lord;
he is our help and our shield.
In him our hearts rejoice,
for we trust in his holy name.
May your unfailing love be with us, Lord,
even as we put our hope in you. (Psalm 33:20-22)

Hope that's just a vague wishing is not hope at all. Real hope requires an object. Something to hope in, or more accurately, someone to trust. Hope, in some ways, connects the present to the future. Hope does not ignore the struggles of life, but acknowledges them.

The hope of Advent is hope in something: God, and the gift of Emmanuel, God with us. We put our hope in God, in grace, in the sufficiency thereof.

We can have hope because God is trustworthy. If ever we need evidence of that, Advent provides it. The long awaited savior has come. We remember the longing, we retell the story, we look toward the nativity—but we know the familiar story. Jesus does come. His birth is not just a vague hope, or even a matter of faithful anticipation. He has come.

In this season, we can invite him to come dwell in us, to be born in us again, to come to our hearts—not just to the world but to us, specifically and personally. No matter how secure we are in our connection with God, there is always room for renewal, for a reminder of unfailing love, even as we put our hope in God anew.

Journal: What specific situation do you need God's help with? Where do you need an infusion of God's unfailing love?

Pray: God, I wait in hope for you;
    you are my help and my shield.
In you, God, my heart rejoices,
    for I trust in your holy name.
May your unfailing love be with me, Lord,
    even as I put my hope in you

December 2

> *Why, my soul, are you downcast?*
> *Why so disturbed within me?*
> *Put your hope in God,*
> *for I will yet praise him,*
> *my Savior and my God. (Psalm 42:5 NIV)*

I love Psalm 42 because it boldly acknowledges that a downcast soul is a thing. We have been through a lot lately, the world feels uncertain and confusing, and we don't know whom to trust. It makes sense that our souls are feeling a bit low.

This passage reminds us that hope is, on one level, a decision. When we put our hope in God, despite our fear, despite our uncertainty, God responds with an infusion of more hope.

Hope is not just a vague longing but a confident expectation, a patient waiting. To hope in God is to trust him.

Trust is a rare thing these days. People mistrust the government, the church, the media, even one another. We're all skeptics. Trust needs a worthy object, and humans are fallible. We cannot put our trust in politicians or even preachers.

When you make a decision put your trust in God, you get something back: hope. God fills you with hope, in spite of your circumstances. He changes your focus, so that you can say, "I will yet praise him" no matter what challenges you face.

Journal: Think about a time when your soul felt downcast. (Maybe that's how you're feeling today.) Is that feeling rooted in Christmas past, or Christmas future? What happens when you gently return your attention to the present moment?

Pray: God, sometimes I don't know who to trust. I feel hopeless, downcast in my soul. Lift me up, God, and fill me with your hope. Help me to be fully present and to notice the gifts that are right in front of me.

December 3

> *The people walking in darkness*
> *have seen a great light;*
> *on those living in the land of deep darkness*
> *a light has dawned. (Isaiah 9:2, NIV)*

Hope, by its nature, seems focused on the future. And yet, to live hopeful lives, we must be fully present. We know we are walking in darkness, but we believe that that the light will shine.

Isaiah's prophesy embodies this tension. Though he is writing about a future event, he states with great faith and hope as if his prophesy has already been fulfilled: the people have seen, the light has dawned.

This time of year, at least in my hometown, it's a physically dark season. The days are short, the sun, reticent. The lack of sunlight can make us feel dark on the inside as well. But we have hope, because the light will soon be dawning. The coming, the Advent, of redemption and rebirth, will happen. It does every year.

What if being present in Advent means letting ourselves slow down, rest, wait patiently (that is, hope)?

Journal: We often take on too many tasks during the holidays. What is one task you could either delegate or simply let go of this year? How might letting it go help you to receive the gift of Christmas present?

Prayer: God, sometimes I feel I am walking in darkness: relationally, spiritually, physically. Fill me with the light of your hope.

Week Two

This week's theme is Peace. Yet we live in a world full of wars, violence and conflict. And our hearts are often restless and anxious, not peaceful at all. How can we experience peace? Is there one relationship or situation in your life that especially needs peace? Make that your focus this week.

December 4

But I have stilled and quieted my soul;
like a weaned child with its mother,
like a weaned child is my soul within me. (Ps. 131:2)

When my son was small, he loved to snuggle. His head on my shoulder, his little fingers absently stroking my arm. No matter what else I needed to get done, I would remind myself to stay present in those moments, knowing they'd be fleeting.

The image of a weaned child is provocative. A nursing baby feels demanding, needy. They root about, trying to take, to get fed. A weaned child though, is content with simple presence, with just snuggling. It's a metaphor for peace.

This week, think about just sitting quietly, cuddling with God. Allow your soul a few moments of stillness, quiet.

Often we say we want peace, but we go after it like a hungry, squalling infant, rooting about trying to satiate our needs. But desperately seeking peace is counter-productive. Instead, imagine ourselves simply sitting in intimate connection with God. When we let go of our demands and seek only presence, peace flows in.

Of course you have a lot to do, and making time for simply being still is hard. But give yourself the gift of a few moments of presence.

Journal: What situation are you facing right now where you need God's comforting presence, like a mother with a young child? What emotions does this image of a weaned child stir up in your heart? In your memory?

Pray: God, today I just want to spend a few minutes being quiet and still in your presence. Show me how to set aside distractions and worries and simply enjoy the gift of time with you.

December 5

Do not be anxious about anything, but in every situation, by prayer and petition, with thanksgiving, present your requests to God. And the peace of God, which transcends all understanding, will guard your hearts and your minds in Christ Jesus.
(Philippians 4:6-7, NIV)

Holidays are a time anxiety escalates. How can we be fully present, rather than worrying about all that lies before us? Anxiety and peace can't coexist.

We miss the gift of Christmas present when we worry about Christmas future. Worry is fear about what hasn't happened yet, the things still on our to-do list or things that are beyond our control: gifts, meals, our décor. Interactions between family members. We're worried that we won't get it all done, so much that we can't enjoy the things we have done. We worry about spending too much, but we keep on buying more stuff.

God's word doesn't just tell us to not worry and leave it there. Thankfully, it offers gentle guidance: practice gratitude and trust. Gratitude is a decision you make, regardless of your circumstances. Gratitude loosens our grip on worry, so we live in the moment instead of the future.

When I feel anxious, I stop and tell myself, "Be here now." It's a simple reminder to be present, so that I can see the blessings, and say thank you. I can let the future worry about itself.

When we express gratitude (thanksgiving) and let God know what we need, we will experience peace that transcends understanding, but is real and comforting.

Journal: Make a list of three things you're anxious about. Then, make a list of three things you are grateful for. How does making each list make you feel? Use your lists in the prayer below.

Pray: God, I am anxious about…. I now give you these things, and ask you to resolve these situations. I release them to your care. I am grateful for… Thank you for the blessings you've given me. Help me to be present and to pay attention to the good in my life, and to remember to practice gratitude.

December 6

> *You will keep in perfect peace*
> *those whose minds are steadfast,*
> *because they trust in you.*
> *(Isaiah 26:3, NIV)*

The Bible defines peace as much richer and more nuanced than simply a lack of conflict. The Hebrew word *shalom* means peace, harmony and completeness (and so much more.)

Shalom is sheer gift, not something we can create by ourselves. And yet, we must choose to receive it. Peace, by it's very definition, can't be forced upon you, or it would no longer be peace.

One commentary notes: "Shalom experienced is multidimensional, complete well-being — physical, psychological, social, and spiritual; it flows from all of one's relationships being put right — with God, with(in) oneself, and with others."[1]

So peace with God means right relationship or reconciliation with God—which our verse for today says comes from a steadfast mind. Peace with others goes beyond the absence of conflict to concern for justice for all. Peace within ourselves, often the hardest to grasp, comes not from our striving but from our openness to God, our focus shifting from our own problems to God's sufficiency—trusting God. When we're at peace with God, we can seek peace and justice for others, and experience peace within ourselves.

---

[1] See https://www.thenivbible.com/blog/meaning-shalom-bible/

Journal: What situation in your life today needs God's shalom? What's one way you can open your heart to God's perfect peace?

Pray: God, I trust you. Help me to be steadfast, focused on you and open to the peace you want to give to me. I accept and receive it.

December 7

So letting your sinful nature control your mind leads to death. But letting the Spirit control your mind leads to life and peace.
(Romans 8:6, NLT)

When the Bible mentions the "sinful nature," what comes to mind? Maybe obvious transgressions like cheating, lying, stealing, or just being mean. Yes, those things are in our nature, so to speak, especially when we think doing them will benefit us in some way.

Our sinful nature can control our minds. Think about how keeping track of our own lies can be mentally exhausting. In the same way, fear and worry, which also spring up out of our flawed human nature, can become our mind's obsession.

It's not a sin to feel anxiety—it's part of being human in the world. (If your anxiety is chronic or debilitating, please seek professional help.)

We need God—because on our own, we're going to struggle to find peace. We'll always battle our embedded fear.

Still, change is possible. Transformation is what God is up to in you. We can cooperate by continually choosing to let the Spirit control our minds—to listen to the voice of love rather than the voice of fear. As we open ourselves to God's perspective and presence, life and peace begin to replace our fear and anxiety. With the Holy Spirit's help, we can live in the present moment, and we can experience peace.

Journal: Today, think about your thinking. What does your inner dialog sound like? Based on that, who controls your mind? Does the voice of fear speak louder, or the voice of love?

Pray: God, help me to listen to the voice of love. Help me to offer control of my mind to your Spirit, instead of my flawed human nature. Guide me toward life and peace.

December 8

But now in Christ Jesus you who once were far away have been brought near by the blood of Christ. For he himself is our peace, who has made the two groups one and has destroyed the barrier, the dividing wall of hostility...
(Ephesians 2:13-14, NIV)

Polarization. It's a word you hear a lot these days. In fact, we've been hearing it for years, as people dig in and hold tight to their positions. Civilized conversation between opposing viewpoints sometimes feels impossible.

Polarization is nothing new. People have been taking sides, and fighting over those positions, for centuries.

Two thousand years ago, the Apostle Paul reminded Jews and Gentiles that Jesus himself had destroyed the barrier of hostility between them. This radical change didn't come easily.

We cannot have peace within ourselves, if we are in conflict with others, or consider them inferior. What feel like irreconcilable differences can only be resolved by Jesus, the one who is himself our peace. But will we allow him to speak into these conflicts, to guide us toward peace?

Journal: What comes to mind when you hear the word "polarization"? Maybe you think of a political, religious, or societal conflict? How could you live at peace with those on the opposite side of that conflict? How can you move toward unity?

Pray: God, please show me today how to be an agent of peace and reconciliation. Help me to love those who see things differently than I do.

December 9

This letter is from Paul, chosen by the will of God to be an apostle of Christ Jesus, and from our brother Timothy. I am writing to God's church in Corinth and to all of his holy people throughout Greece. May God our Father and the Lord Jesus Christ give you grace and peace.
(2 Corinthians 1:1-2, NIV)

Dear brothers and sisters, I close my letter with these last words: Be joyful. Grow to maturity. Encourage each other. Live in harmony and peace. Then the God of love and peace will be with you.
(2 Corinthians 13:11, NLT)

Paul's letters, which comprise about half of the New Testament, often begin and end with a blessing: grace and peace to you. May the God of love and peace be with you.

Grace and peace are a gift, given by a God who loves you. How can we access that gift? Paul offers advice: be joyful, grow up, encourage others, live in harmony. Easy to say; sometimes hard to do.

"Grow to maturity." It seems a curious directive, but important. My kids are in their twenties, and as they launched into independence, they would sometimes say, "adulting is hard." It is. Growing to maturity is not an easy road. But growing up spiritually leads us to greater peace. How do we engage in this growth?

These are interconnected goals: joy, maturity, encouragement, harmony. When we choose joy, we will experience peace. When we prioritize our own growth, choosing the path to maturity, we experience God's presence. Filled with that presence, we can encourage others, which will transform our relationships and lead us to live in harmony with others. We will not be worried or regretful, but fully present with others, God and ourselves.

Journal: No matter our age, we always have room to grow. What is one small thing you could do today to take a step toward growing to maturity?

Pray: God, help me to pay attention to opportunities to grow spiritually. Fill me with your grace and peace today.

December 10

I'm leaving you well and whole. That's my parting gift to you. Peace. I don't leave you the way you're used to being left—feeling abandoned, bereft. So don't be upset. Don't be distraught. (John 14:26-27, MSG)

Advent focuses us on the birth of Jesus, his first coming. But Jesus promised at the end of his life that he would come again. And in the meantime, we would have the Holy Spirit to comfort us, and a peace unlike any other to dwell in our hearts.

This Advent, many of us are feeling deep loss—whether of a job, a loved one, or just longing for the way things used to be. Jesus promises that he will not leave us like that. He doesn't abandon us when we are in pain. Instead, he leaves us a gift of peace in our hearts, despite our circumstances.

But sometimes, life gets in the way. Our worries and fears block us from experiencing the peace that Jesus wants to give us. Our busyness becomes a barricade. But when we focus on being present, we can receive the gift of his peace.

Today, pay attention to the people around you: your family, friends, even strangers you see as you shop, work, or go about your day. How can you give them the gift of peace that Jesus has given to you?

Journal: What barriers get in the way of you experiencing the peace that Jesus gives? What is one step you can take to begin dismantling those barriers?

Pray: God, I so often get distraught and upset, worried and fearful. Today, fill me with your peace. Let me be well and whole, and fully present in each moment.

Week Three

The traditional theme for Advent's third week is love. This poor, overused word describes a wide range of feelings. For example: I love chocolate, I love your new outfit, I love this book, I love this musician's songs, I love my kids, I love God. In each of these contexts the meaning is different. This week, focus on the unconditional love God has for you. Where do you need to experience and receive that love?

December 11

*The Word became flesh and blood,
and moved into the neighborhood.
We saw the glory with our own eyes,
the one-of-a-kind glory,
like Father, like Son,
Generous inside and out,
true from start to finish.
(John 1:14, MSG)*

In Advent, we remember the birth of Jesus; we put ourselves in the story to anticipate his coming, as if it were brand new. God no longer a far-off deity, but a flesh and blood child who will grow into a man, who lives in our neighborhood.

There's this lovely paradox in John's description of Jesus as "glorious," because we know his human birth was so humble. He was born to parents who were poor, ordinary. But have you ever met someone who despite their humble circumstances, shines with a light of God's generosity and truth?

What if you could be that person? Jesus came to bring salvation, and to show us how to live. What would it take to live "generous inside and out, true from start to finish"? In other words, to be the same person all the time. To consistently live the values Jesus came to teach us.

Journal: At this time of year, we can confuse overspending with generosity. But what does generosity on the inside, generosity of spirit, look like? How can you be generous today? Could you do it without going shopping?

Pray: God, thank you for loving me enough to come to earth, to become flesh and blood. You are not distant, but someone who understands the struggle and joy of what it means to be human. Help me to live like you lived: generous and true.

December 12

Anyone who claims to live in God's light and hates a brother or sister is still in the dark. It's the person who loves brother and sister who dwells in God's light and doesn't block the light from others.
(1 John 2:9-10, MSG)

This week's theme is love. As a child I sang in church: "They'll know we are Christians by our love, by our love…"

Looking around these days, the song feels quaint and even ironic. Christians are often known by their hate, or at least, their opposition. Faith has gotten tangled in our politics, and our divisions seem wider every day. Even our views on medicine and science (from the pandemic to climate change) have taken on a political charge. Mistrust runs deep. Logic seems hard to find.

I want to be the kind of Jesus follower who is known by my love. For everyone. Here's the rub: that means I'm invited to love people that I disagree with. How do I love the very people I'm accusing of being hateful? Because if I don't show love to those people, I'm no better than they are.

What would happen if we actually loved? This week, focus on what it means to be a conduit of love. Receive God's love, and let it flow through you to those around you: harried store clerks, the people you live with, your co-workers, strangers you encounter. Even, and especially, let love flow to people who annoy you.

Journal: Am I a person who claims to live in God's light, but am actually still living in the dark? Who is God inviting me to love right now?

Pray: God, I want to dwell in your light, and not block others from seeing and experiencing it. Help me to love others, even if they seem hard to love. I can only do it with your help—may I be a conduit of your love today.

December 13

My beloved friends, let us continue to love each other since love comes from God. Everyone who loves is born of God and experiences a relationship with God. The person who refuses to love doesn't know the first thing about God, because God is love—so you can't know him if you don't love.
(1 John 4:7-8, MSG)

When something is new, enthusiasm abounds. It's in the daily slog, the long haul, that things get harder. Today's scripture exhorts us: "let us continue to love…" The continuing, though struggles, pain, disappointment—that's the real test of love.

We struggle to love others because we are trying to give from a place of emptiness—as futile as attempting to pour water from an empty cup.

Being "born of God" is more than just praying a certain prayer, accepting certain beliefs. In the tradition I grew up in, getting people "across the line of faith" was the stated goal. But the Bible offers something richer (and more challenging): "let us continue to love."

The continuing happens not by sheer effort, but by staying open to God in a way that we are filled, rather than depleted. Slowing, listening, receiving the love that we could never manufacture or even think of on our own.

And then, taking that abundance and sharing it by being present with people—really listening, not thinking about the past or the future, not checking your phone, but really listening.

When we are filled with love, we can love others.

Journal: A soul surrounded by love responds to God by loving others. What fills you with God's love? Is it seeing the beauty of nature? Meditating on God's truth? Simply taking time to sit and be still? Write down three things that fill you with God's love. Do one of them today.

Pray: God, I want to continue to love, but honestly, sometimes I get tired and depleted. Fill me with your love today. Help me to slow down and receive your love, so that I can love others.

December 14

My dear, dear friends, if God loved us like this, we certainly ought to love each other. No one has seen God, ever. But if we love one another, God dwells deeply within us, and his love becomes complete in us—perfect love!
(1 John 4:11-12, MSG)

I'm a nature girl, no matter what the season. All winter, I continue to run and hike outside, no matter the weather. I notice God's handiwork and feel love in the gift of it. I also have a high capacity for solitude. I'm rejuvenated by time alone—and if it's time alone outdoors, all the better. God speaks to me in silence, and in the natural world.

But God invites us to receive his love, then share it with others. And when we do, "his love becomes complete in us."

What a crazy idea. If God's love can be made complete (by us!), then is it "incomplete" to begin with? God is perfect, but our experience of God is incomplete, inaccessible, outside of our giving and receiving love from others.

God takes a wild risk by giving his children a crucial role to play: we are the completers of love.

We cannot experience all God wants to give us unless we love others—and others will miss out on the fullness of God's love if we don't offer them that love.

We're invited to step into the flow of God's love, to let God dwell deeply within us, and at the same time, share that love and experience it more profoundly.

Journal: Respond to the idea that loving others completes God's love. How does this responsibility and opportunity feel to you?

Prayer: God, help me to love others today. Show me someone who feels like something is missing in their life, who feels incomplete. Help me to notice and respond to that person, to show your love to them.

December 15

*What marvelous love the Father has extended to us! Just look at it—
we're called children of God! That's who we really are.*
(1 John 3:1, MSG)

In the almost three years since everything changed, anxiety and depression have become their own pandemic. Job loss, isolation, uncertainty—these weigh on us, crushing our self-esteem, or at least making us question our worth.

In these uncertain times, worry about the future (Christmas or otherwise) can overwhelm. And yet, we're invited to remember who we are: children of God.

Our identity is not in our job, our accomplishments or the accomplishments of our children. Rather, our identity comes from God's love. That love is not something we earned or can strive for. It is simply "extended to us." God is the initiator, and we are simply children who can bask in that love.

You are a child of God, and the light of God's love shines in you. Take some time today to be present, to notice that light, to bask in God's marvelous love and let it shine within you.

Journal: The holidays can be a time of conflicting emotions or even sadness. Check in with yourself: how are you feeling today? Take some time to simply be present, and focus on the marvelous love your heavenly Father has extended to you.

Pray: God, thank you for your love. Help me to live in the truth that I am your beloved child.

December 16

There is no fear in love. But perfect love drives out fear, because fear has to do with punishment. The one who fears is not made perfect in love.
(1 John 4:18, NIV)

Love is not mushy or sentimental, but courageous. It takes courage to love.

If we are to live in love, we must resist its opposite. You may think of hate as love's opposite, but hate springs from love's true opponent, which is fear.

What keeps me from being present, especially in a busy season? I must daily make a choice: what voice do I listen to: the voice of love, or the voice of fear?

The voice of fear threatens scarcity, uncertainty, even doom. The voice of love reminds us that God's provision is abundant and sufficient, that God's presence is a gift we cannot buy, but also cannot lose.

The Bible's most-repeated command is "do not be afraid." But just trying to muscle up enough resolve to cast aside our fear is almost impossible. We must have something to replace it with, something to fill the space that fear now occupies.

Letting go of fear can be scary in itself, because it feels like letting go of control. If I stop worrying, what will happen?

The promise in today's scripture: perfect love (that is, love from God) drives out fear. This is not a call to perfectionism, but an invitation to lean into perfect love. God's love floods our hearts, rinsing fear away.

Journal: Without judgment, write down three things you are afraid of. No matter how irrational those fears may be, simply write them down and look at them. Be still for a moment, and imagine God driving those fears away, filling that space in your heart with perfect love.

Pray: God, my fears are stubborn. I'm inviting you to drive them out, to let your perfect love flood my heart and fill it. Help me to love courageously today.

December 17

"For this is how God loved the world: He gave his one and only Son, so that everyone who believes in him will not perish but have eternal life. God sent his Son into the world not to judge the world, but to save the world through him."
(John 3:16-17, NLT)

Have you ever received a gift that blew you away? Not necessarily expensive, but just utterly thoughtful. Do you remember how it felt to receive it?

Imagine receiving a gift like that, and in response, pulling out your wallet to pay the person. Or your phone, to Venmo them. "This is great, thank you. Let me give you some money." The giver would likely feel insulted.

A gift is just that: a gift. We often make our gift giving transactional: guessing how much to spend on each person based on what they will spend on us. But that's not the kind of giving God does.

The true gift of Christmas, of course, is Jesus. God sent him, but this does not imply reluctance on Jesus' part. He chooses to come, not to judge but to save. He is a messenger of love, and the embodiment of love.

Perhaps this week you are buying last minute gifts, making preparations for holiday meals or gatherings. As you do, think about God's gift of love to you. Take a moment to slow down, even for a minute, and to simply feel grateful for that abundant love.

Journal: In the tradition you grew up in, was God's love really a gift, or one you felt you had to earn? In what ways do you still attempt to earn God's favor? What do you think it means to believe in Jesus?

Pray: God, thank you for sending Jesus to give me the gift of life. Help me today to embrace and rejoice in the free gift of your presence in my life.

Week Four

Just the word, joy, stirs in our hearts a longing. C.S. Lewis described joy as the very longing itself for joy. "All Joy reminds," he wrote. "It is never a possession, always a desire for something longer ago or further away or still 'about to be.'" [1] This week, rather than trying to pin down joy, focus on the longing for it, and how that longing itself brings you a joyful anticipation.

---

[1] Lewis, C.S. *Surprised by Joy: The Shape of My Early Life*. New York: Harcourt Brace Jovanovich, 1955, 78.

December 18

> *²⁶ In the sixth month of Elizabeth's pregnancy, God sent the angel Gabriel to Nazareth, a town in Galilee, ²⁷ to a virgin pledged to be married to a man named Joseph, a descendant of David. The virgin's name was Mary. ²⁸ The angel went to her and said, "Greetings, you who are highly favored! The Lord is with you."*
> *²⁹ Mary was greatly troubled at his words and wondered what kind of greeting this might be. ³⁰ But the angel said to her, "Do not be afraid, Mary; you have found favor with God.*
> *...³⁸ "I am the Lord's servant," Mary answered. "May your word to me be fulfilled." Then the angel left her. (Luke 1:26-30, 38, NIV)*

In order for Jesus to be born, God needed to find a woman. Not just any woman. A woman who would be willing to take a huge risk, a huge step of faith.

It's easy to miss, but key: Mary was highly favored before she said yes. She hasn't even heard why the angel is there, but right off the bat, he tells her: God is crazy about you.

God was present with her, and favored her, before she agreed to this highly inconvenient divine assignment. It just might be possible that God feels the same about you: that you're loved, favored—not because of what you do, but because of whose you are.

Mary's elderly cousin Elizabeth was pregnant. According to bible history, God had not spoken to his people through a prophet, an angel, or anyone, for about 400 years. The Old Testament ends, and there is 400 years of silence. Then an angel shows up, and both a virgin and a menopausal woman are pregnant. Things are apparently about to get very interesting.

In order to be present, to find joy, we must choose to listen to the voice of love, and respond to it. The voice of love is the counterpoint to all the messages of fear and shame: I'm inadequate. I'm alone. I'm scared.

The voice of love, on the other hand, says:
You are highly favored.
The Lord is with you.
Do not be afraid.

Journal: Sit for a moment, and focus on these words; *do not be afraid.* What are you feeling fearful about right now, in this moment, on this day the week before Christmas. What situation does this bring to mind? Where does it resonate in your life? What are you afraid of?

Pray: God, I am your servant. Thank you for your favor and your presence.

December 19

*You will show me the way of life,
granting me the joy of your presence
and the pleasures of living with you forever.
(Psalm 16:11, NLT)*

What brings joy during the holidays? For me, it's relationships: family and friends around table or Christmas tree, or moments of quiet reflection and prayer with God.

For years, I took family holidays together for granted. I even stressed about it. But as my kids get older (and sometimes spend holidays with the family of their significant others), I realize what a gift simple presence truly is. Over the last few years, holiday meals have shape shifted. Pandemic-related restrictions sometimes kept us from gathering. Holiday travel is tougher.

This year, take a moment to turn your attention from the tasks, and cultivate gratitude for the fact that you can be with the people you love. And if you're not able to be with those people, remind yourself that God is always present with you, regardless of your circumstances.

The gift of Christmas present comes when we can experience the joy of God's presence in our lives. We do not have to earn or strive, but simply slow down, and pay attention. God will show us the way. But we must set aside our hurry and worry.

Our kind heavenly parent wants to give us the joy of presence, and will show us the path to that sweet communion. It begins, I think, with slowing down to listen, to pay attention, to focus on the present moment.

Journal: In these busy days, it's easy to feel disconnected from God. Write down three things you can do today to slow down, focus and receive the joy of God's presence. Notice what you are longing for.

Pray: God, show me the way of life.
Grant me the joy of your presence.

December 20

> *[39] A few days later Mary hurried to the hill country of Judea, to the town [40] where Zechariah lived. She entered the house and greeted Elizabeth. [41] At the sound of Mary's greeting, Elizabeth's child leaped within her, and Elizabeth was filled with the Holy Spirit. [42] Elizabeth gave a glad cry and exclaimed to Mary, "God has blessed you above all women, and your child is blessed. [43] Why am I so honored, that the mother of my Lord should visit me? [44] When I heard your greeting, the baby in my womb jumped for joy. [45] You are blessed because you believed that the Lord would do what he said."*
> *(Luke 1:39-45, MSG)*

Mary embarks on an adventure like no other: to bear and raise the Son of God. In the face of mystery, Mary chooses joy, rather than fear.

I love this chapter of Luke because it's so radical. It was written into a patriarchal culture, to an audience that did not value women. And yet, both Mary and Elizabeth speak God's truth with remarkable assurance and strength. There is no man-splaining allowed—in fact, Elizabeth's husband John has literally been muted, struck dumb for his doubt.

Elizabeth feels the movement of her unborn child (who would grow up to be John the Baptist) and recognizes it as a jump for joy. The text connects joy with the Holy Spirit. She knows Mary's news before her young niece can speak a word. She affirms Mary's faith. She uses the word "blessed" three times: twice to describe Mary, once to describe her child. And why is she blessed? Because of her faith: "because you believed that he Lord would do what he said."

We're often seeking blessing, striving for God's favor. But Mary has found it simply by believing.

Journal: We'll read Mary's response tomorrow, but for now, focus here. Where are you seeking God's blessing? What situation do you need to reframe and believe that God will do what he promises?

Pray: God, sometimes my doubts destroy my joy. Today, I want to believe that you will do what you said.

December 21

> *And Mary said,*
> *I'm bursting with God-news;*
> *I'm dancing the song of my Savior God.*
> *God took one good look at me, and look what happened—*
> *I'm the most fortunate woman on earth!*
> *What God has done for me will never be forgotten,*
> *the God whose very name is holy, set apart from all others.*
> *His mercy flows in wave after wave*
> *on those who are in awe before him.*
> *(Luke 1:46-51, MSG)*

Mary bursts forth with bold, prophetic words, in a song traditionally referred to as the Magnificat, Latin for magnifies, as in "My soul magnifies the Lord."

What if joy comes not from demanding satisfaction from God, but from magnifying God? If we focus on adoration and praise, putting all other things into perspective, God becomes bigger, more prominent, more central.

When we experience God's favor, God's mercy—we can be filled with joy. Mary could have worried: learning you're pregnant before you're married would have been reason for a bit of stress, right? But instead she names her blessings, and as her praise flows toward God, it comes back multiplied magnified, intensified. You can see in Mary's words echoes of Psalms and other Scriptures, but she's woven them with her own experience and thoughts to create her own original praise song. She's in the flow of joy.

Journal: Write down three things you are grateful for. Take time to reflect on them, to thank God for them, to let them pull you into the flow of joy. Let God's mercy flow on you in wave after wave. Write about what this experience feels like, what God says to you in response to your gratitude.

Pray: God, thank you. Your mercy is flowing on me—help me to recognize it, to step into the flow of your goodness, to be aware of your power and love all around me.

December 22

And there were shepherds living out in the fields nearby, keeping watch over their flocks at night. ⁹ An angel of the Lord appeared to them, and the glory of the Lord shone around them, and they were terrified. ¹⁰ But the angel said to them, "Do not be afraid. I bring you good news that will cause great joy for all the people. ¹¹ Today in the town of David a Savior has been born to you; he is the Messiah, the Lord. ¹² This will be a sign to you: You will find a baby wrapped in cloths and lying in a manger."
¹³ Suddenly a great company of the heavenly host appeared with the angel, praising God and saying,
¹⁴ "Glory to God in the highest heaven, and on earth peace to those on whom his favor rests."
(Luke 2:8-14, NIV)

In the most improbable way, love came to all people. A baby born to a poor young couple, welcomed by a handful of common laborers. Angels announce his coming, not to kings or rulers, but to ordinary folks. Great joy, the angels sing, to all the people. Not just the privileged or elite.

In your ordinary life, you may not be serenaded by an angel choir. You might, instead, be surrounded by squabbling children, or gossipy co-workers, or cranky family members. But the angels' message is relevant today, to whatever you face: do not be afraid. Good news. Great joy. For you.

No matter who you are, no matter how you're struggling. Jesus' coming is good news for you—because he comes bringing unconditional love, hope, peace, and yes, joy.

Journal: What are you afraid of right now, in this moment? What worries or uncertainties threaten to steal your joy? Make a list. Then next to each one, write, do not be afraid. Acknowledge the fear, but then release it. Let God hold your fears, and replace them with joy-inducing good news: you are loved, and the gift of Christmas present is yours for the taking.

Pray: Jesus. Savior. Messiah. I welcome you into my heart, into my life. Clean out my fears and replace them with the joy of your good news.

December 23

So they hurried off and found Mary and Joseph, and the baby, who was lying in the manger. [17] When they had seen him, they spread the word concerning what had been told them about this child, [18] and all who heard it were amazed at what the shepherds said to them. [19] But Mary treasured up all these things and pondered them in her heart. [20] The shepherds returned, glorifying and praising God for all the things they had heard and seen, which were just as they had been told.
(Luke 2:16-20, NIV)

This part of the Christmas story is a study in contrasts. The shepherds show up, then start posting on social media. Okay, well, the first century equivalent. They spread the word, telling everyone they can about this miraculous event.

The shepherds are talking to everyone, and people are amazed. Then the shepherds noisily return, praising God. I wonder if those who'd heard their news wanted to visit the baby as well, curious about a messiah born in such humble circumstances.

And in the middle of the joyful chaos, Mary chooses her own brand of joy: a quiet pondering. An awe-filled treasuring. To treasure something is to recognize its value. In the events of that night, she may have felt overwhelmed or uncertain. But she stops and reminds herself to be present, to treasure and ponder.

This Christmas Eve, your life may be quiet, or it could be chaotic. Take a moment, somewhere in the middle of all you have going on, to treasure up all that is treasurable in your heart, and to let go of everything else. Release the regrets of Christmas past, hand over the fears for Christmas future, and simply breathe. Be fully present in this moment, this Christmas Eve. Ponder in your heart the gift: you are deeply loved.

Journal: Christmas often flies past in a whirl of activity. List two or three things that you experienced this Advent that you want to treasure and ponder. What gave these things value?

Pray: Thank you, God. For the gift of your presence, for the opportunity to ponder and treasure all that you are to me, and all that you've given me. Thank you for loving me.

December 24

*For a child is born to us,
a son is given to us.
The government will rest on his shoulders.
And he will be called:
Wonderful Counselor, Mighty God,
Everlasting Father, Prince of Peace.
(Isaiah 9:6, NLT)*

Merry Christmas!

Today, simply let the gifts of Christmas present—hope, peace, love and joy—fill your heart. Be fully present with God and others.

Made in the USA
Monee, IL
10 November 2022